THE
60-SECOND
CHRISTIAN

Other Word Books by Gary R. Collins

Christian Counseling

The Joy of Caring

Beyond Easy Believism

The Magnificent Mind

THE 60-SECOND CHRISTIAN

GARY R. COLLINS

WORD BOOKS
PUBLISHER
WACO, TEXAS

A DIVISION OF
WORD, INCORPORATED

Library of Congress Cataloging in Publication Data

Collins, Gary R.
　The 60-second Christian.

　1. Christian life—1960–　.　I. Title.　II. Title:
Sixty-second Christian.
BV4501.2.C6426　1984　　　248.4　　　84-13103
ISBN 0-8499-0450-1

Printed in the United States of America

CONTENTS

1

THE 60-SECOND CHAPTER

One of the biggest mysteries in all of the universe is why God put inexperienced young couples in charge of parenthood. Young fathers don't know anything about changing messy, smelly diapers. Young women, just out of the hospital, aren't rested enough to get up in the middle of the night for breast feeding, and husbands can't help because they tend to lack the necessary equipment.

In time, the parents get used to having a baby around the house, but then the kid starts to change. Babies become toddlers who, by definition, are messy eaters and inclined to get into everything. Toddlers become preschoolers, and eventually these little dynamos become junior highers who labor under the delusion that they are grown up, intelligent, and sophisticated. Parents and school boards assume in vain that the high schools will teach their students to understand science and English, but instead the kids learn most about sex, drugs, talking on the phone, and the need for loud noise that sometimes masquerades under the name of music.

In view of all this can you understand why the average father in this country apparently spends less than one minute every day in close contact with his children? According to some unknown researcher, the kids in most homes spend an average of thirty-seven seconds talking to their fathers during each twenty-four-hour period. Statistics like that make excellent illustrations for Father's Day sermons, and are guaranteed to arouse parental guilt.

In me, this statistic also arouses skepticism. No one knows for sure how much time fathers spend with their children, and even if we did know, would such information be of any value? How much time we spend with our kids is important, but what also counts is what we do with the time together.

Not long ago, a creative writer wrote a book titled *The One Minute Father*. I was skeptical. How, I wondered, can anybody be a parent in one minute?

But that wasn't the author's point. Instead, he

argued that many useful things can be done in sixty-second periods. The book described some one-minute actions that could be used to discipline children, to get their attention, to enlist their cooperation, and to help them feel good about themselves.

This got me thinking. A lot of significant things can and do happen in less than sixty seconds.

In less than sixty seconds you can go through a radar trap and experience the flashing red light in your rear view mirror.

It takes less than a minute to break your leg in a skiing accident or to plow into somebody at an intersection.

You don't need a course in sex education to know that a sperm and egg can get together and start a pregnancy in a lot less than sixty seconds.

And if you're like me, you've made some statements in your lifetime that may have taken only a few seconds to say but might have tied you up for years. "I'd love to help" can be said in two seconds (try it) but these four little words can lead to hours and even months of tedious work. And think of the implications of "I do!"

We Americans, and our Canadian cousins to the north, like things that can be done quickly. Our lifestyles involve instant replays, fast foods, immediate credit, and quick diets that occasionally work. A lot of things can be done quickly and that isn't always bad.

Some people—me for example—like books that can be read quickly. This one is an example. According to an unbiased and nonscientific survey, taken by me in my house and with me as the only subject, each of the chapters in this book can be read in about sixty seconds. If you don't believe me, time yourself on chapter 2. It begins with the story of a person who became a Christian—in less than sixty seconds.

2

THE 60-SECOND CHRISTIAN

The Discussion du

There once was a young man who wanted to become a Christian.

As a young boy, he was told that he lived in a Christian nation (whatever that means) and he assumed that everybody who wasn't Muslim or Jewish must be a Christian.

But one day he met a friend who knew something about the Bible and whose life, in some way, seemed to be different. The two got to talking about religion and the friend made the remarkable statement that God loves individual people. According to the Bible, He made us and He gave us freedom. He could have created robots who couldn't think and who could be wound up and made to do whatever God wanted.

But He didn't.

1. Know the Lord
2. Positive Approach

11

Instead, God made people and even gave them the freedom to ignore Him or to turn against Him if they wanted.

And that is exactly what has happened. Even moral people have fallen into sin (if you'll pardon an old-fashioned word), and that sin is what separates us from God. Try as hard as we might, there is no way—according to the Bible—that we can work to get rid of our sin and buy into God's favor.

The young man had never heard anything like this and to be honest, he was disturbed and a little confused. If God gave us freedom and let us sin, why should He get upset when we gave in to a little temptation? If God really cares about us, why won't He let us work our way into heaven?

The answer, so the young man discovered, is that God has provided another way—the only way that works. In spite of what the popular self-help books say about human potential, no one on this earth is good enough to buy his or her way into God's favor. So God sent His Son, Jesus, to die on the cross to take punishment for our sins.

Then He rose again. That's what the Easter story is all about.

No one has to work or do religious acts to get rid of sin. All we have to do is believe that Christ is God's Son who forgives sin and wants to guide our lives.

12

The young man really wondered if this was in the Bible so his friend showed him:

"God . . . loved us so much that even though we were spiritually dead and doomed by our sins, He gave us back our lives again when He raised Christ from the dead. . . . Salvation is not a reward for the good we have done, so none of us can take any credit for it. It is God Himself who has made us what we are and given us new lives from Christ Jesus. . . . If you tell others with your own mouth that Jesus Christ is your Lord, and believe in your own heart that God has raised Him from the dead, you will be saved."

Then the friend quoted what probably is the best known sentence in the Bible: "For God loved the world so much that He gave His only Son so that anyone who believes in Him shall not perish but have eternal life."

"I believe this," the young man said quietly, and then the two friends prayed. In simple words they told God that they believed.

That is how the young man became a Christian.

It wasn't anything spectacular.

It took less than sixty seconds. But it began a whole chain of events in the young man's life.

The Bible verses are from Ephesians 2:4,5,9,10; Romans 10:9 and John 3:16.

Confess with your mouth Jesus is Lord, in your heart God raised from the dead will be saved.

Gods great love for us we are dead in our transgressions.

not by works, we are God's workmanship should do good works

13

3

THE 60-SECOND BUMPER STICKER

Christians, as everyone knows, have a tendency at times to go to church. Our young man, who could now be called the Sixty Second Christian, decided to give it a try one Sunday, so he rolled out of bed at the crack of dawn, 10 a.m., and made his way to the nearest place of worship.

He almost didn't go in.

The parking lot, he discovered, was lined with cars bearing bumper stickers. Bright, colorful, and sometimes gawdy, the messages were fascinating and as meaningful as the inscriptions on weather-beaten tombstones.

The first, he had seen before: "Jesus Saves!" As a new Christian he was beginning to understand what that meant, but it hadn't made much sense before. The Datsun people used a similar slogan to sell cars, but they had never been able to get their slogan to form into a neat little cross like this:

JESUS
A
V
E
S

The Sixty Second Christian had a little trouble making sense of the next bumper sticker: "Honk if you love Jesus!" Why do that? he wondered. Was that some kind of a Christian ritual that he would hear about in church?

Maybe they could also explain what it meant to "Tithe if you love Jesus!" But it would take some doing, our hero concluded, to explain why anyone would want to stick a message like that on the back of a car where it could distract drivers, most of whom wouldn't have the foggiest idea as to what it meant. The Sixty Second Christian wasn't sure either.

Even more confusing was the "Warning!" on the bright yellow sticker that proclaimed "In case of the Rapture, the driver of this car will disappear." What's a rapture?

And so it went: "Born Again Club!" "Jesus Makes House Calls!" "Do you need a faith-lift?

Call on Jesus!" "God Gives Gusto." "Read the Bible: A Chapter a Day Keeps the Devil Away." "From womb to tomb, Jesus lifts the gloom."

What kind of people stick messages like these to the bumpers of their cars? Probably sincere people, the Sixty Second Christian concluded. Maybe they are people who think these messages do some good by alerting others to the gospel.

But what if nobody understands? Are these cute little sayings any different than the beer advertisements or the sexually suggestive slogans that we read on other bumpers? Would the Sixty Second Christian have become a follower of Jesus if he had paid much attention to these "witnessing tools"?

He thought about this as he passed the last car and moved toward the door of the church. Aren't there better ways to let people know you're a Christian?

Some day the Sixty Second Christian would learn what Jesus said in His most famous sermon: "Let your *good deeds* glow for all to see, so that they will praise your heavenly Father."

Isn't that another way of saying that actions speak louder than bumper-sticker words?

Those sermon words of Jesus can be read in Matthew 5:16.

16

4

THE 60-SECOND GREETING

Sometimes we modern people like to use old words that sound nice but don't have much meaning. Professors, for example, like to encourage their students to be "scholarly," which is another way of saying, "You had better read another stuffy book or two before you hand in your term paper." Salesmen sometimes talk about "business ethics" which could be another way of saying, "The right way is my way." You've probably heard people talk about "quality control," "respectability," and even "patriotism," but few know much about the meanings of these words.

In the church, one of our favorite terms is "fellowship." According to the dictionary, this refers to an association of friendly people who have similar tastes and interests. Others, who come into contact with such a fellowship, are supposed to feel welcome.

But this doesn't always happen, especially when you make your first visit to a strange church.

The Sixty Second Christian, for example, was a little hesitant as he left the parking lot and approached the door of the church. But there at the entrance was an official church "greeter" waiting to welcome all strangers into the local fellowship.

The greeter was a short, balding, effervescent man who wore a plastic carnation on his lapel and a smile on his face to match. He was friendly. There was no doubt about it. But after his sixty-second greeting he shifted the visitor over to an usher and turned to greet the next arrivals.

The Sixty Second Christian felt pretty lonely when they seated him all by himself in the third row. He didn't feel any better when he was supposed to sing "choruses" that he didn't know, tried in vain to find Ezekiel in the pew Bible, and heard the preacher ask all visitors to stand so they could get a little green visitor's ribbon and a brochure about the church.

The Sixty Second Visitor stayed seated.

He sat through a sermon that had three points (but no explanation for the messages on the bumper stickers). He let his mind wander, fought to keep awake, and decided that the morning "message" was boring, long, and not much related to his struggles and concerns in life.

After the closing prayer, the room erupted into animated conversation as the regular worshipers turned to their friends for fellowship. Like participants at a cocktail party, the people divided into little talking-groups, oblivious to the visitor standing by himself in the third row.

Nobody said anything to the stranger.

Nobody seemed to notice as he slid silently past the chattering saints and out the door.

Even the bald man with the plastic carnation was nowhere to be seen. Apparently he had gone someplace for fellowship too.

5

THE 60-SECOND MEDIA CHURCH

The following Sunday, the Sixty Second Christian decided to stay in bed while he went to church. In less than sixty seconds he turned on the television set and laid back, ready to watch some of those controversial television preachers.

They put on a good show. There were no bald men with plastic flowers here. Everybody was beautiful, with big smiles and stylish wardrobes. The music was superb—just like the Saturday night television specials—and the sets were overflowing with real plants and flowers. This was a lot better than sitting in the third row of a church, trying to find Ezekiel.

The sermons were better too. There were no three-point outlines or theological discourses here. Nobody talked about suffering, death, or

s this
what God
ought

injustice. There was no mention of disturbing things like commitment, service for others, or self-denial.

1. "All you need is a positive attitude," said one preacher. "You can do all things if you have the right mind-set."

2 "God doesn't want you to have financial problems," said another.

3 "God doesn't want anybody to be sick," proclaimed another who then closed his eyes and prayed an emotional prayer for the sick people who were supposed to be touching their television sets as a "point of contact" with God.

One enthusiast encouraged the viewers to take "just a minute—sixty seconds" to write a check and address an envelope. In return he promised that God would reward abundantly—with a return far higher than any money-market account. For an extra five dollars the speaker (not God) would give a copy of his latest book of sermons.

The Sixty Second Christian didn't want to be critical. These television people seemed so sincere, even when they advertised their books, records, rallies, and forthcoming Christian-celebrity "love boat" cruises. But everything seemed too slick, too wonderful.

Being a Christian, it seemed, was not much different than being a nonbeliever. There was glam-

or, success, and maybe even fame—especially for those who looked pretty, could write a book, or were able to get on one of those television shows.

Was this the Christianity that Jesus taught? Even as he watched from his bed, the Sixty Second Christian sensed that something was wrong. The media people might be sincere (there was no reason to think they weren't), but they seemed so smooth, so distant, and so unreal. And they didn't provide much opportunity for personal contact with new believers like the Sixty Second Christian. To learn more about Jesus and to find Christian friends he probably would have to turn to something other than a television set.

It took him less than sixty seconds to turn off the picture and go back to sleep.

II Cor. 11:13-15

GALS. 1:1-9

Heb.5:11-14

Philip. 3:1-2

Perfect Christ is

6

THE 60-SECOND CARING

Some people in this world are mechanical geniuses. They can fix anything—stereos, toasters, bicycles, cars, even computers. This has to be a God-given knack, like the ability to carry a tune, to learn French, to grow plants that don't die, or to keep your hair from falling out or turning gray before you reach fifty. Some can do it. Most can't.

One cold morning, the Sixty Second Christian was driving to work, paying minimal attention to the traffic or stoplights, and singing along with some sad song on the car radio.

Then it happened.

The car quit.

There was no warning or thumping or smell of burning rubber. The old beast just died and refused to budge, even in response to a serenade of blaring horns coming from a growing line of impatient drivers.

As you know, there is only one way to deal with such embarrassing situations. The Sixty Second Christian got out of his car, put up the hood and peered at the engine. He had no idea what to look for. In terms of mechanical skills, he had none. He knew that he was "all thumbs" and had been ever since he first arrived in this world. Looking under the hood would tell him nothing about the car, but he hoped that his distress would attract the attention of some mechanical genius who could diagnose the problem, fiddle with a wire or two, and get the car rolling again.

It was a long wait. People don't stop to help much in our society. There's too much suspicion that drivers in distress are really muggers, waiting, even in broad daylight, to rob any "Good Samaritan" who might be naïve enough or stupid enough to stop. Sometimes the stoppers are the muggers.

But the two college students who pulled over to help weren't thieves or robbers. Regretfully, they also weren't mechanics, but at least their car was still working. They offered the Sixty Second Christian a ride and took him to a place where he could call for help.

That's all. Nobody got attacked, kidnaped, brainwashed, or mugged. The two rescuers dropped off their passenger, waved good-bye and took off without even giving their names. The whole rescue operation took about five minutes.

Nobody knows if the college students were Christians, but apparently they had learned the one lesson that, according to Jesus, sums up all the Old Testament. We call it the golden rule: "In everything do to others what you would have them do to you."

Jesus lived like that. In fact, He was the One who came up with the golden rule in the first place. There must have been many times when He put the golden rule into practice—and it only took a minute or two of His time.

Could that old principle work today with one's children, spouse, fellow workers, neighbors, or even with the boss?

The Sixty Second Christian decided to try it in his own life.

He wondered if others might misinterpret his motives. Sometimes that happened.

He noticed, too, that others appreciated his efforts to help, and that made him feel good.

One day he took a minute to write these words on a card. It is still taped near the bathroom mirror so he can remind himself to put the one-minute rule in practice:

"I will treat others the same way I expect to be treated."

The golden rule can be found in Matthew 7:12, (NIV).

Therefore

Math 5:20   Keep the Law
II Cor. 1:3-4

7

THE 60-SECOND
ENCOURAGEMENT

When he treated others kindly, the Sixty Second Christian began to notice how people were reacting.

Some were embarrassed. They didn't know how to react to acts of kindness and they gave the impression that it might be better if they could be left alone.

Some were suspicious. *What's that guy up to?* they wondered. What's he trying to prove or what does he want? A few even resisted all offers of help.

But most people responded positively and some even put the principle to work in their own lives.

One day the Sixty Second Christian found a little note in his mailbox. It only had two sentences, and probably took only about sixty seconds to write.

"Thanks for helping me today. Your concern really lifted my spirits, and I wanted you to know how much you helped."

The person who wrote that note has probably never heard of Barnabas. He is mentioned a few times in the New Testament, but not because he was a great preacher or a super-Christian. His main claim to fame was his tendency to encourage others.

Maybe Barnabas took an old quill pen and occasionally scratched out messages of encouragement on parchment. More likely, he told people that he appreciated them, and looked for opportunities to make encouraging statements, without being insincere or gushy.

The Sixty Second Christian grew up in a home like that where encouragement was modeled. His parents knew that a lot of children live with incessant criticism. Some fathers (and mothers) bark more than the family dog, and words of encouragement and praise are as rare as a snowstorm in July. These parents, like some married couples, have become modern spies, always looking for something to criticize.

Wouldn't it be better to look for things that are right? Doesn't it make better sense to look for reasons to express praise, appreciation, and encouragement? Even as a child, the Sixty Second

Christian had learned that families get along better with less tension, conflicts get resolved more smoothly, and people feel better about themselves when they make it a habit to give frequent compliments and words of encouragement.

The two-sentence note was enough to remind the Sixty Second Christian that he too could encourage others. He decided to give at least one compliment a day.

The office secretary was first. Everyone knew she was an old sourpuss, probably older than Barnabas. But she made good coffee and the Sixty Second Christian took a minute to tell her so. The poor woman nearly died of shock. Nobody had complimented her on anything for years and in spite of her surly response, the compliment pleased her and aroused a flicker of warmth deep inside.

No one thought much about the changes that came to the office in the weeks that followed. The morale just seemed to get better, and the atmosphere of perpetual complaining tended to clear. People started to compliment and encourage each other—all because one inconspicuous person decided to look for something positive in others and to give at least sixty seconds of encouragement to someone, once every day.

It's not easy to believe that something so simple

could bring any kind of a change. But the only way to know is to try it yourself. Try it for a month, and if you can't handle it that long, just try it for a few days.

Look for the good in others. Write someone a note, say what you appreciate, thank the person for helping you, say something good about the person—and keep it short. Other people are easily embarrassed.

That's what happened to the Sixty Second Christian. He became the Sixty Second Encourager and everyone felt good about it—especially him.

JOSEPH → Son of encouragement

You can read about Barnabas in Acts 4:36, (RSV). Several Bible passages tell us to encourage one another. See 1 Thessalonians 5:11, for example, or look at Hebrews 3:13; 10:25. Philippians 4:8 instructs us to let our minds dwell not on what is wrong in others, but on that which is good, admirable, and praiseworthy.

Note of Encouragement
Compliment

Exhorting call along side
appeal

8

THE 60-SECOND ENCOUNTER

Have you ever met someone famous? If so, you probably discovered that well-known people are not usually interested in talking to strangers. Sometimes there is a handshake, a meaningless comment or two, and the encounter is over—all in less than sixty seconds.

A lot of our contacts with people are like that—brief and sometimes so insignificant that we don't remember them very long. I wonder how many husbands or wives have no recollection of the first meeting with the one whom they later married? I wonder if you or I will meet some person today whose influence, although we might not recognize it at the time, could indelibly change the course of our whole lives. This doesn't happen often, but it happens.

31

After work one evening, the Sixty Second Christian was idly browsing in a religious bookstore, skimming the titles and occasionally taking a minute or two to pull something from the shelf and flip through the pages. He didn't even see the young lady in the aisle until he literally bumped into her—right between "Biblical Archeology" and "Christian Sex."

I'll not bore you with details of their apologies and initial conversation, but somehow they got to the topic of church and the young lady told the Sixty Second Christian about the people with whom she worshiped.

The emphasis at her church, she said, was not on money or buildings or programs. The focus was on worship and spiritual growth, the emphasis was on people, and the believers tried to keep an awareness that they were followers of Jesus.

The Sixty Second Christian had visions of plastic boutonnieres and green "visitor" ribbons. But he also liked the idea of having contact with other Christians (the lady in the bookstore could be a good start) so he agreed to at least think about meeting with a "fellowship" (there's that word again) group from the lady's church.

In that group the Sixty Second Christian found something he could never get from television or stuffy church services. There was caring—about him as a person, and about each other. There was a sincere desire to share each other's burdens, to pray for one another, and to see whether the Bible really touches our lives.

The Sixty Second Christian learned something that is almost un-American.

① People need people.

There is no virtue in rugged individualism, in handling problems all by ourselves, or in trying to "bloom where you are," all alone. Christian status seekers and prima donnas are as lonely, insecure, and self-destructive—perhaps worse—than their secular counterparts. The real way to mature and to grow in this life is to be involved with a group of other ordinary believers.

If he had stayed in the bookstore long enough, the Sixty Second Christian could have read about this in a very old book—the Bible. No Christian can say to another, "I don't need you." The Bible states that we are all parts of "the body of Christ," like the hand, eye, and brain are all parts of the physical body. If one part hurts, the whole body feels it. If one part feels good, the whole body tingles.

At the time of his encounter in the bookstore, the Sixty Second Christian could never have known that his involvement with other believers, even imperfect believers, would start a growth spurt in his progress toward personal and Christian maturity.

Do you suppose God might have arranged this encounter?

The Bible compares the "body of Christ" to the physical body in 1 Corinthians 12:12–27.

Psalems 139:

9

THE 60-SECOND WORSHIP

For several years, the Sixty Second Christian had heard God referred to in a very familiar way. After all, if God is supposed to be our friend, why not call Him "the man upstairs," "our big daddy in the sky" or some other term of endearment? Didn't a lot of people do that?

One day he heard someone suggest that terms like this are, to say the least, flippant.

"I don't think those who use these terms mean any disrespect," the Sixty Second Christian protested. And that was probably true. Like most people, including him, they had very likely never thought much about what God is really like.

Many people think that God must be like Santa Claus—far away, somehow able to know if we've been bad or good, and willing to give us presents if we keep out of trouble. Others seem to think that God is like a little genie who gives us what we want if we know a few magic words.

Other people think that God the Father is like their earthly fathers. Thus, if you had a good father, you have a good view of God, and if you had a bad father, you assume God isn't too good either.

Someone told the Sixty Second Christian about a book an Englishman had written several years ago after the Second World War, when so many people in Europe had suffered and died. The experience had left many with feelings of bitterness. Some admitted that they were angry at God, but others, like the Englishman whose name was J. B. Phillips, had come to appreciate the greatness of God in a new way. Phillips titled his book *Your God Is Too Small.*

The Sixty Second Christian wondered if his view of God was too small. Like a lot of people, he believed that God was loving. But isn't God also wise, so that He knows what is best for us? Isn't He also all powerful, completely fair, absolutely perfect, holy, and so knowledgeable that He knows our names and even our secret thoughts? If God is something less than this, then He isn't God. Phillips is right: Most of us have a view of God that is too small. We don't give much time or attention to God because we don't think of Him as being all that powerful, influential, or important.

The Sixty Second Christian hit on an idea for learning about God. Each evening, before going to bed, he opened his Bible to the Psalms and began reading until he came to one statement about what God is like. Then he stopped and thought about what he had read. (He also made a pencil mark in his Bible so he would know where to continue reading on the next night.)

One night he read that God is good.

Another night he read that God is faithful.

He read that God is compassionate.

He found out that God is forgiving.

He also learned to thank God for each of these characteristics. It became a little form of personal worship—without any choirs, organs, or distracting stained glass windows.

The Sixty Second Christian thought about one of these traits as he turned off the light each night. Most mornings he discovered that the same thought was often one of the first ideas to pop into his mind after he turned off the alarm. Had his mind been meditating on this characteristic of God all night?

When he told somebody about this, the Sixty Second Christian was criticized and told that he had come up with a gimmick that didn't mean anything. But over a period of weeks he discovered that he was growing in his awareness of God and in his appreciation for God's character.

And . . . many nights, as he read in the Psalms he found a trait of God to ponder in less than sixty seconds.

10

THE 60-SECOND CONFESSION

What do you suppose is the most out-dated and forgotten word in the English language?

Some of Shakespeare's words might be good candidates for answering this question. Maybe we could try some like "forsooth," "wherewithal," or "perambulator."

Or we might try "confession."

Depending on your past, that word could bring all kinds of ideas to mind: stuffy little confession booths in a church; overweight preachers droning on from a prayer-book; parents trying to get you to admit to something you didn't do.

Or confession might bring memories of insensitive teachers, keeping the whole class after school because some creative and bored individual did something harmless like draining the aquarium. Teachers apparently are taught in college that the way to get someone to "confess" is to keep everybody in after school. It never works. Everybody in the class is mad, except the guilty person and he—or she, sits there looking mad like everyone else, trying to hide the fear of being caught as the culprit. When all the kids know who is guilty, everyone "boils with righteous indignation," wondering if tattling really is a sin.

Is it any wonder that we don't like confession? *speak & sanc-ti*

But the Bible keeps using the word. The writers of that Good Book knew that confession has a way of cleaning up our minds, and making us feel at peace inside.

Some of these thoughts went through the mind of the Sixty Second Christian after he exploded at work one morning. The issue wasn't all that big, but he was tired, impatient, and not inclined to take a lot of silly chatter from other people. So he said what he thought—in no uncertain terms.

There is an old theory that claims it can be good to blow up periodically. This is supposed to let out our hostilities and help us feel better. But it isn't a very good theory. It takes less than a minute to tell somebody off, but you can feel bad for the rest of the day, or longer. The resentment that builds up hurts you more than anyone else, and the blow-up doesn't really help anyone.

So the Sixty Second Christian decided to apologize.

"I'm sorry!" he said in one-sixtieth of a minute. "I lost my cool and I didn't mean to hurt you. Would you please forgive me?" Then he added a word of appreciation, saying something good about the person he had criticized earlier in the morning.

Have you ever noticed how hard it is to make such an admission? Have you also noticed how liberating it can feel to apologize?

Maybe that's why God tells us to confess our sins. When we confess to Him, He forgives us and wipes away all traces of the wrongs that we have done.

When we confess to others—like a close friend or a spiritual leader—we experience inner healing, and are more inclined to pray.

Confession, of course, doesn't do any good if we are not truly sorry, and really do not want to change. But if we want to change, with God's help, we can. That's the kind of desire that makes confession really effective.

The Sixty Second Christian once heard of a way to confess in sixty seconds. Whenever he became aware of something he had done wrong, he told God about it immediately. He said he was sorry, asked God to forgive, and then asked that the

41

Holy Spirit would control his life and help to keep him from such sins in the future.

This is sort of like breathing—breathing out the sin in confession, breathing in God's full presence by asking Him to spread throughout our whole lives. It takes less than a minute, but the whole process is like a cleansing breath of unpolluted, clear fresh air.

Maybe confession isn't such an irrelevant word after all. It makes more sense than "forsooth" or "perambulator."

You can read some interesting statements about confession in 1 John 1:8 and 9; and in James 5:16.

Isaiah 59:1,2   Phil 1:1 and 2 I

Rom. 10:9,10 confess with thy
                          mouth

I Tim. 6:11-13

John 18: 33-38

11

THE 60-SECOND SERVE

Not long after he first became a believer someone told the Sixty Second Christian that he should be reading the Bible. That seemed like a reasonable suggestion, especially for someone who was wanting to know more about God.

The Sixty Second Christian had friends who read their Bibles often and seemed to know about its contents. He admired their dedication and their knowledge. He wondered about the people who claimed to be Christians and discussed the Bible, but were too busy to read it.

It didn't take long for the Sixty Second Christian to learn that some parts of the Bible are easier to understand and more interesting than others. He was glad he started at the beginning of the New Testament and read about the life of Jesus. A lot of it was familiar, of course, but some of the teachings seemed pretty radical.

There was a time, for example, when two of Jesus' followers came to make a request of Him. They must have been "momma's boys" because apparently they were scared to ask for themselves, so momma said what they (and probably she) wanted.

"When we get to heaven," she began, "can my two sons please sit next to your throne, one of my boys on your right, the other on the left?"

Today we would call that a blatant grab for power, and even the other people in Jesus' little group got pretty upset when they heard about the request.

But Jesus handled it graciously.

He began by telling them they couldn't have what they wanted, but then He went on to state the obvious: in this world, the important people are those who have power, positions of prominence, and prestige. It also helps if you have a lot of money and are able to live a lifestyle that lets people know that you are successful. That's what we value most in our society—success. (Those two momma's boys would make good Americans.)

Then Jesus said something radical. Christians shouldn't value things like that. "Whoever wants to become great among you must be a servant. . . .

Anyone wanting to be the greatest must be the least—the servant of all." Jesus even stated that the top people in His kingdom are willing to be slaves.

Is it any wonder that modern people don't read the Bible or take Christianity seriously? Didn't servanthood and slavery go out with emancipation? Isn't it more patriotic to believe in civil rights? Who wants to be a servant?

Nobody.

But isn't that what makes Mother Teresa great? Isn't that a characteristic that we admire—in others? Isn't that what Jesus Himself came to demonstrate—in contrast to the status-seeking and smug superiority of the religious leaders of His day?

Jesus came to serve.

The Sixty Second Christian knew that this little Bible story was calling for a radical change in both his thinking and the way he dealt with others. He wasn't even sure how he would go about being a servant.

Then he remembered something that Jesus once said to His followers. "Love one another. As I have loved you, so you must love one another." Love, said Jesus, was to be the mark of a Christian. Seeing that love in action is how people recognize Christians. It took less than a minute to read these words of Jesus, and re-read them.

All sin is rooted in selfness
All virtue is springs out of love

The Sixty Second Christian knew a lot of believers who weren't very loving. Some were more inclined to gossip and to argue than to love.

But Jesus told us to love. That wouldn't be easy, but the Sixty Second Christian determined to try to love people, as Jesus loved. He wasn't sure how he'd start. But to act like a servant would be a good practical place to begin. Somehow he suspected that the Bible would give him more guidance about this if he kept reading. But in the meantime he decided to look for opportunities to be helpful. The next time somebody needed a ride, wanted help with a move, or could use a hand with a heavy load, the Sixty Second Christian was ready to assist. These were only little ways to serve—but once he started to think like a servant he began to see how many ways he really could reach out and help somebody.

You can read about the momma's boys in Matthew 20: 20–28. See also Mark 10:45, Luke 6:31. For Jesus' commandment to love one another see John 13:34; 15:12, (NIV).

12

THE 60-SECOND SEMINAR

It only took a few weeks for the Sixty Second Christian to discover that a lot of Christian people like to attend seminars. The topics tend to vary, he had been told, but some issues—like family living, parenting, time-management, self-esteem, spiritual gifts, positive thinking, and even sex—come up repeatedly. And for reasons that nobody can understand, there seems to have been a special interest in seminars dealing with temperaments—and youth conflicts.

The Sixty Second Christian had never attended a seminar like these, but he concluded that they must be important. Some of his Christian friends talked about seminars all the time, took pride in their big seminar notebooks, and even went back to the same old seminars again and again. When did they have time to put their knowledge to work? he wondered. Was it possible that these sincere people found it easier to hear the "word" than to apply it to their lives?

As far as he could surmise, the Sixty Second Christian concluded that the seminar leaders were often attractive, interesting, humorous, and inclined to be from out of town. Some even saved time and travel expense by appearing on film.

Much of what they said was basic psychology, couched in religious language, and made acceptable to the audience because the lectures were sprinkled liberally both with Bible verses and heart-rending stories.

The Sixty Second Christian decided that the time had come to see one for himself. It took less than a minute to fill out the registration form and pay the fee. It would take a lot longer to sit through the meetings.

It didn't take long to discover that the leader was a good speaker whose words and illustrations captivated the audience. And there could be no doubt about the fact that he did say some good things about coping with the anxieties of life.

"To handle pressure," the speaker proclaimed, "you should be realistic. Recognize that some things can't be changed.

"Manage your time carefully. Don't agree to do

more than your time permits. Since there never is enough time to do everything, set some priorities. Make a list of things to do, start with the most important, and go from there.

"Don't procrastinate. That only adds anxiety and puts you under pressure.

"If you make a mistake, admit that you were wrong. People who can admit their follies and laugh at their own imperfections will never have a nervous breakdown.

"Recognize that you have both strengths and weaknesses. We all do. If you face yourself honestly, and realize that you are a valuable creature in God's sight, you can develop a healthier self-image.

"When pressures build, talk things over with a friend. And be willing to listen to others when they are under pressure."

Most of this was helpful, but the Sixty Second Christian had heard it before.

But he hadn't heard what came next.

In less than a minute, the speaker said, "Jesus gave us two rules for living. They come right out of the Bible: 'Love the Lord your God with all your heart, soul, and mind'; and 'Love your neighbor as . . . yourself.'"

That, concluded the Sixty Second Christian, won't be easy without some help, but he wanted to make sure that he applied what he had learned to his life. So he left the seminar concluding that he would have to find out how to get that help. Could he learn to pray?

The two rules Jesus gave for living can be found in Matthew 22:37–39.

Last Chap. notes
Gal. 5:13 +14
Letu 19:18
Matt. 5:43-44, 46, 48
19:19
22:37-39

13

THE 60-SECOND PRAYER

Have you ever heard the old hymn, "Sweet Hour of Prayer"?

The Sixty Second Christian had heard it sung at a funeral once, but the idea of spending an hour in prayer seemed incredible. It was even wilder to think that such an activity could be "sweet."

Prayer, it seemed, was like the weather. It is something that a lot of people talk about but nobody does anything about. Prayer is ignored by most people—at least until they get into a bind.

The Sixty Second Christian had no idea how to talk to God—even for a minute, much less for a "sweet" hour. So to get some help with this, he wandered into the religion section of the public library to see if anybody had written a book about prayer.

To his surprise, there were hundreds of books on the subject. The Sixty Second Christian wondered why there were so many books on prayer but no seminars. Maybe prayer wasn't as popular or as important as stress management.

It was an interesting idea—but he put it out of his mind, picked out a book at random, and took it home to read.

As he read, the Sixty Second Christian discovered that Jesus wants us to pray. He didn't give any set formulas for praying, didn't say we had to kneel or pray out loud, and didn't even say we had to pray for an hour.

In fact the Sixty Second Christian learned to pray by simply talking to God, just as he would talk to any other friend, in one-minute sentences.

He had already learned that prayer sometimes involves saying thanks to God for what He is like and for what He does.

Sometimes the Sixty Second Christian confessed his failures and frustrations to God and asked for both forgiveness and help.

At times he asked for things, and told God about his needs, desires, and hopes.

As the weeks went by, he discovered that he was talking to God more and more frequently—in one-minute sentences.

He said "give me" a lot less—and he found himself saying "make me . . ." a lot more.

He found his attitude changing so that he was less inclined to treat God like a magic genie, and more willing to ask that God's will would be done.

Sometimes he forgot to pray very much, and he noticed that his life on those days was more hectic and less peaceful.

One day he noticed that his prayers sometimes went longer than a minute, or two. He had begun with sixty-second prayers but now prayer had become a part of life, almost like breathing.

Would even *he* someday find it possible to spend a "sweet" hour in prayer? Maybe the idea wasn't old-fashioned and crazy after all.

But it was obvious that even an hour in prayer would have to be made up of sixty-second prayers.

14

THE 60-SECOND THANKS

Do you remember the story about the ten lepers? They were a sickly bunch whose disease was incurable and so contagious that they were quarantined and required to roam on their own outside the city.

One day, these men heard that Jesus was passing by, so they called out and begged for healing.

When Jesus brought an instant cure they jumped for joy and nine of them ran off to tell their friends.

But one of them, a foreigner, took the time to say "thanks."

The Sixty Second Christian read about this one day. He wondered how often he said thanks—to God, or to others.

He knew that it was easy to be critical. It didn't take any effort to criticize waitresses, telephone operators, secretaries, relatives, or others who sometimes were inefficient, insensitive or impolite.

But if it takes little effort to criticize, would it take much more effort to say "thanks"?

There once was a scientist who spent his life studying how people respond to stress. In a book published years ago, this scientist, a man named Hans Selye, proclaimed that one attitude is essential for mental health. If you want peace of mind, he wrote, if you want to be fulfilled, secure, and successful in life, then learn to be grateful.

The Sixty Second Christian had read about this someplace, but it had never occurred to him that it could be put into practice. He didn't know at the time that the same idea is sprinkled all over the pages of the Bible: Christians are supposed to be thankful people—and not just when they pray over the turkey on Thanksgiving Day. They are supposed to be thankful all the time—even when things go wrong.

That was one of the toughest, but most important, lessons for the Sixty Second Christian to learn. He could understand why the one leper was ecstatic about being healed. It's easy to say thanks when things are going well. But it isn't easy and it doesn't even make a lot of sense to say thanks when we hurt or when things aren't going right. It isn't easy to say thanks when we feel angry, and are more inclined to be sarcastic. And what does one do when he doesn't feel thankful, or when—like the nine lepers—he forgets?

The Sixty Second Christian was learning that people who are serious about their religion sometimes are called to do things that aren't easy.

And nobody said that the Christian life would be easy.

That's one reason why we need Jesus, and each other: to help us to be thankful when we don't feel like it.

"I'm always with you," Jesus once said.

The Sixty Second Christian was thankful for that.

But the more he thought about it, the more the Sixty Second Christian realized that he was thankful about other things as well—things that he often took for granted.

He could be thankful for his sight, his health, his freedom, his car (even with the dents), his friends, and his job—in spite of the boss.

Thankfulness, he discovered, can become a way of life. It lifts our spirits.

And it sure is a lot healthier than griping.

Look at Luke 17:11–19; 1 Thessalonians 5:18; Hebrews 12:15.

15

THE 60-SECOND WITNESS

At times, I suppose most of us have wondered how our great-grandparents would react if, by some cruel fate, they were brought back to spend a few hours living in these last days of the twentieth century.

They probably wouldn't live very long. If the smog and fast drivers didn't kill them, the speed of our lifestyles would. And they probably would be overwhelmed and dumbfounded by our modern airports.

The Sixty Second Christian thought about this when he went to meet a friend who was "stopping over" for a brief visit on his way to Europe. Darting past the bustling crowds and waiting lines, the Sixty Second Christian made his way through the security system and headed out to the gate to meet his friend.

But he was stopped on the way.

First there was the young damsel selling flowers, as a come-on to her religion.

Then there was the man who was giving out little pieces of paper with cute headings and stories that the busy people in the airport didn't have time to read.

One person appeared seemingly from nowhere, proclaimed that he, and God, loved people in airports, and wanted them to hear about his spiritual laws.

The Sixty Second Christian had to keep going, but he wondered if this was what the Bible meant when it told Christians to be Christ's witnesses.

As he waited for the plane, the Sixty Second Christian struck up a conversation with a lady who was waiting to meet her daughter. The daughter's marriage had broken up and the mother was deeply distressed.

As they talked, the Sixty Second Christian found himself telling this lady about Jesus. They talked about the love of God, about His forgiveness, and about things that the Sixty Second Christian had been learning during the previous weeks. There was nothing contrived, embarrassing, or artificial about their conversation. Like

Jesus, and Paul, who talked freely and casually about their faith, the Sixty Second Christian told about his life and how Jesus was a friend especially to people who were hurting.

The conversation about Jesus didn't last long—perhaps no more than a few minutes—but it had a tremendous influence on the lady waiting at the gate.

Later, as he visited with his friend, the Sixty Second Christian thought about these experiences in the airport. He had no real criticism of the flower lady, the paper man, or the one who wanted to share the laws. These were people who had the guts to approach strangers and to talk about religion, even in a busy airport.

Wasn't that more admirable than being a silent believer and saying nothing?

But wouldn't it be better to let God open conversations so we can talk about Jesus without gimmicks?

16

THE 60-SECOND TAKE-OFF

After his friend said good-bye, the Sixty Second Christian decided to wait until the plane was airborne.

The take-off was beautiful. The gleaming 747 seemed to lift effortlessly off the runway and up into the sky. Its wheels folded under the silver body and the plane climbed gracefully until it was enveloped by the feathery clouds that floated over the airport.

For some reason, the Sixty Second Christian was in a reflective mood as he walked back to the car.

He thought about his friend in that plane. As the passengers rode to Europe, they would pass about ten ground miles every sixty seconds. Every minute, they would get ten miles closer to their destination. The journey of several thousand miles would move along, sixty seconds at a time.

Life is like that, the Sixty Second Christian thought. We can think about the past and plan for the future, but we live in the present moment. Minutes of caring, encouraging others, worshiping God, confessing, serving, praying, giving thanks, and witnessing—all add up to a lifetime of useful, fulfilled, God-pleasing living.

The Sixty Second Christian had once read about a man named John. Apparently he was one of Jesus' closest friends.

John knew that it wasn't easy to be a Christian. He knew that we tend to stumble and flounder as we walk through life. He reminded people that Jesus understands and is always willing to help and to forgive.

But John once gave a profound piece of advice to anyone who wants to live a fulfilled life. The advice can be read in far less than sixty seconds:

"Anyone who says he is a Christian should live as Christ did."

Could anything be shorter—and more precise?

Living minute by minute as Christ did, is the way to take off on the journey of a lifetime.

The Sixty Second Christian slid into his car and

turned on the ignition. Slowly, he drove toward the cashier's booth ready to pay the parking fee and swing out onto the freeway.

But apparently everyone else was going home too, and the Sixty Second Christian found himself in a massive traffic jam.

There are many things in life that can be done in sixty seconds, he thought as the car slowed to a crawl.

But getting out of a traffic jam isn't one of them.

The scripture verse used in this chapter is 1 John 2:6.

17

THE 60-SECOND REFLECTION

While he moved through the late afternoon traffic, and later pulled into his driveway, the Sixty Second Christian could not have known what his friend was thinking as the plane flew freely out over the Atlantic.

The friend had noticed how the Sixty Second Christian had changed.

His language was better than it used to be.

He was less sarcastic and no longer so inclined to be cocky and insensitive.

He seemed to be kinder, happier, more patient, and less up-tight.

Maybe it is strange that the Sixty Second Christian hadn't noticed most of these changes—although others had.

He didn't claim to be perfect or to have it all

together. He was well aware of his own struggles, and willing to admit his imperfections.

He didn't claim to have found a new religion, but he did say that he had found a new friend: Jesus.

"Could that old idea still be relevant today?" the airplane passenger wondered as he leaned back in the comfortable seat in that modern jet.

How could he have known that the Sixty Second Christian was slowly, minute by minute, becoming like the person described in the Bible centuries ago?

The description is in a letter written to a sixty-second Christian named Timothy. "Don't waste time arguing over foolish ideas," the letter stated. Instead, "practice being a better Christian, because that will help you not only now in this life, but in the next life too."

And don't let people look down on you. Instead, "set an example for the believers in speech, in life, in love, in faith, and in purity." Put your "hope in God," Paul tells Timothy, "who richly provides us with everything for our enjoyment. . . . Do good, be rich in good deeds and . . . be generous and willing to share."

Others had begun to see that the Sixty Second Christian was learning a life-changing lesson: The Christian's purpose in life is to be like Jesus.

That is a powerful idea to think about. It can be read in only a few seconds, but reflecting on it takes much longer. Putting it into practice takes a lifetime—a minute at a time.

And think about this: We are each on this earth so we can be like Jesus.

Is there any good reason why you, too, couldn't become a Sixty Second Christian?

These encouraging words to Timothy can be found in 1 Timothy 4:7–8, (TLB), and 12, 6:17, 18, (NIV).

THE
60-SECOND
POSTSCRIPT

A

THE 60-SECOND QUESTIONS

Once upon a time (this week to be exact), there was a reader who picked up a book titled *The Sixty Second Christian* and read it.

"Should I tell anyone I've read this book?" the Sixty Second Book-Reader wondered.

"Would my friends who line their shelves with theology books and cuddle up to Strong's *Systematic Theology* still love me if they knew I had read a book like this? Would they think I'm an airhead?"

Could it be interesting, and even fun, to discuss this little volume and kick around its ideas with others who appreciate the struggles of the Sixty Second Christian?

This could be done at church, the Sixty Second Book-Reader thought, *or we could get together over coffee some evening.* Without debating further, the

Reader got on the phone and set up the discussion party.

A few days later, the friends all got together and spent more time than they had intended, discussing questions like the following:

What are some things people can do in sixty seconds or less?

Chapter 2 tells you how to become a Christian. Do you agree with the author? Look up the Bible verses mentioned at the end of the chapter.

Think of some creative Christian bumper-sticker ideas. (Maybe you could start a new business.)

Be honest: have you ever put a bumper sticker on your car? How do you suppose other people have reacted to this? Is there a better way to point people to Jesus?

How do you react to the last two sentences in chapter 3?

What does the word "fellowship" mean? Have you ever had an experience like the Sixty Second Christian had in chapter 4? Is your church like that? How can it be different?

What do you think about those famous television preachers? Do you agree with the Sixty Second Christian? Why?

Can people today still live by the Golden Rule?

Have you ever tried it? Why? What happened? Are you more of a criticizer or an encourager? Could you start writing notes of encouragement? Who would get the first ones?

Look up the Bible verses at the end of chapter 7. What might this have to do with you—and your friends?

Do you agree that people need people? Why? How does this apply to you? What does it say about your church?

What is wrong with calling God "The Man Upstairs"?

The Sixty Second Christian wondered if his evening thoughts about God were only a gimmick. What do you think? Have you tried this?

What do "forsooth" and "perambulator" mean? (If all else fails, you can look these words up in the dictionary—but you probably don't care that much.) Try defining "confession"— that's a more important word to know.

When was the last time you confessed something to God or to another person? How did it feel? Is confession really good for the soul?

Is the breathing idea at the end of chapter 10 really practical? Look up the Bible verses. How do they apply?

The Sixty Second Christian "wondered about

the people who claimed to be Christians and discussed the Bible, but were too busy to read it." How do you feel about that?

Read Matthew 20:20–28. How could this apply to your life and career in the 1980s?

The Sixty Second Christian knew a lot of Christians who weren't very loving. Do you? How can you be more loving? Be specific.

Chapter 12 talks about managing stress. Can this apply to your life?

Share some of the experiences you have had in attending Christian seminars.

How often do you pray? How long do you pray each time? Have you ever spent a "sweet hour" in prayer? Can the Sixty Second Christian's approach to prayer help your prayer life?

When was the last time you said thanks to God—or to some other person?

Is it really possible to be thankful when things go wrong? Look at Luke 17:11–19 and 1 Thessalonians 5:18.

When He lived on earth, Jesus talked to people about spiritual things as He walked in the streets. How do you think He would approach people today in airports? Does this say anything about His followers—like you?

Read these words from chapter 16: "Anyone who says he (or she) is a Christian should live as

Christ did." How does that apply to you? Try to be practical in your answer.

Read the last two sentences in chapter 17. How do you respond?

Is there any reason why you couldn't get together with a group of friends who have read this book, and discuss questions like these? Maybe you could dream up some questions that are better.

You could be a Sixty Second Christian, a Sixty Second Book-Reader, and a Sixty Second Discussion Starter—all at the same time.

That would take more than sixty seconds.

But it could be worth the effort.

B

THE 60-SECOND READING LIST

Perhaps you want to read more about the ideas presented in the preceding chapters. If so, try to find some of the following books. You can read this list in sixty seconds, but the books will take longer—even for speed readers.

Collins, Gary R. *Beyond Easy Believism*. Waco: Word, 1982.

Foster, Richard J. *Celebration of Discipline*. New York: Harper & Row, 1978.

Little, Paul. *Know Why You Believe*. Downers Grove, Illinois: Inter-Varsity, 1968.

Oglvie, Lloyd John. *Praying with Power*. Ventura, California: Regal Books, 1983.

Pinnock, Clark H. *Set Forth Your Case: An Examina-*

tion of Christianity's Credentials. Chicago: Moody, 1967.

Stott, John R. W. *Basic Christianity.* Downers Grove, Illinois: Inter-Varsity, 1958.

Tozer, A. W. *The Knowledge of the Holy.* New York: Harper & Row, 1961.